Pool

Written in association with the
British Association of Pool Table Operators

D1584366

Produced for A & C Black by

Monkey Puzzle Media Ltd
48 York Avenue, Hove, East Sussex BN3 1PJ

Published in 2010 by

A & C Black (Publishers) Ltd
36 Soho Square, London W1D 3QY
www.acblack.com

Third edition 2010

Copyright © 2010, 2001, 1995 BAPTO

ISBN 978 1 4081 1413 1

A CIP catalogue record for this book is available from the British Library.

Note: Whilst every effort has been made to ensure that the content of this book is as technically accurate and as sound as possible, neither the authors nor the publishers can accept responsibility for any injury or loss sustained as a result of the use of this material.

This book is produced using paper that is made from wood grown in managed, sustainable forests. It is natural, renewable and recyclable. The logging and manufacturing processes conform to the environmental regulations of the country of origin.

Acknowledgements
Thanks to Bob Blakeborough for his assistance with the text. Many thanks to Steve Daking and Heidi Daking.
Cover and inside design by James Winrow and Tom Morris for Monkey Puzzle Media Ltd.
Cover photograph © Shutterstock
Textual photographs © Grant Pritchard 5, 7 (bottom), 9 (top), 11, 12, 13, 14, 15, 16, 18, 19, 20, 21, 23, 24, 25, 26, 27 (top), 28, 29, 30, 31, 45, 57; © Shutterstock 7 (top), 27 (bottom); © Rob Pearce 9 (bottom), 35, 37, 38, 41, 49, 52; © Bob Blakeborough 33, 42; © Getty Images 47, 51, 60, 61.
Illustrations by Dave Saunders.

The British Association of Pool Table Operators, PO Box 4734, Shrewsbury, SY1 9FQ

KNOW THE GAME is a registered trademark

Printed in China

Note: Throughout the book players and officials are referred to individually as 'he'. This should, of course, be taken to mean 'he or she' where appropriate.

CONTENTS

FOREWORD

*K*now *the Game Pool* has been compiled under the guidance of The British Association of Pool Table Operators (BAPTO). BAPTO was formed in 1975 in order to harmonise the activities of those involved in the supply of pool tables to the licensed trade. BAPTO is responsible for the promotion of the game and for the standardisation of the rules of pool in the UK.

THE ASSOCIATION

Though a non-profit-making organisation of mainly commercial companies, BAPTO has a vested interest in the development of pool and in the popularity and strength of the game. BAPTO is delighted with its progress since it was established over 30 years ago, and wishes to thank all those who have supported the association and its work.

A GAME OF SKILL

Pool is a game of skill and tactics. It is an exciting game, where opponents use their expertise to outwit each other. As with all sports, the only way to gain experience and a clear knowledge of the game is with plenty of practice. Bad habits are easy to pick up but much more difficult to lose. The tips and hints provided in this book are intended to help you improve your game, avoid bad habits, and enable you to appreciate and practise the best of what you see in others.

Know the Game Pool focuses mainly on 8-ball pool (the most popular game in the UK). At the end of this book you will find a section on several simple fun games which can also be played on a pool table (see pages 56–61). Pool techniques apply to all of these games.

THE GAME

Each game of pool is played by two players, or two teams usually not exceeding two players per team. In team games, the partners make alternate 'visits' to the table.

You can find out more about BAPTO by logging on to the website at www.bapto.org.uk.

Pool is played with 16 balls. The white ball (cue ball) is slightly smaller than the other balls – 14 object balls and the 8-ball black. The object balls are seven balls numbered 1 to 7 and seven numbered 9 to 15, or seven balls of one colour (usually red) and seven of another colour (usually yellow).

The purpose of the game is for a player to pocket all of his or her

Pool is an exciting game, but players need to keep their cool to stay in control.

object balls and then the 8-ball black. A player's group of object balls is not established until the game is underway (this is explained on pages 24–25).

BLACKBALL RULES

Most major competitions are now played to 'blackball' rules (see pages 54–55). However, as many leagues are played following the rules of 8-ball pool, these are included in this book.

Work at fully understanding the game and the skills required. Avoid copying others, who may have picked up some bad habits.

EQUIPMENT

The basic equipment required to play pool includes a pool table, a minimum of two cues, a full set of balls, a rack and some chalk. The quality of equipment and sizes of tables and cues may vary, but the basic requirements remain the same for casual or competition games.

THE TABLE

The playing surface of the table, called the 'bed', is normally made of slate and is covered traditionally by a wool, nylon or a wool/nylon mix cloth. The 'nap' of this cloth – the direction in which the fibres lie when smoothed down – runs from the 'D' end of the table to the bottom cushion. A 'gabardine' or napless nylon cloth is used occasionally to provide a very hard-wearing cloth. Some players feel this creates a faster game, but with less control, particularly of the cue ball.

The bed of the table is surrounded by six cushions and six pockets. The cushions are made up of a wooden frame with the flat-faced rubber cushions attached to it, covered in the same material as the bed of the table. Pool tables have flat-faced cushions so that the bounce of the object balls, which are normally 5.1cm (2 inches) in diameter, and the cue ball, 4.8cm (1.9 inches) in diameter, is consistent. The size of the pockets should be 1.6 to 1.8 times the diameter of an object ball at the point where the ball drops off the table.

TABLE MEASUREMENTS

Pool tables vary in size, with overall external measurements of 1.8m x 1.06m (6 ft x 3 ft 6 inches) to 2.1m x 1.2m (7 ft x 4 ft). The height of a pool table is 79–86cm (31–34 inches). The 2.1m (7-ft) tables are generally used in major competitions. Larger tables are too big for most locations and do not offer as interesting a game as competition tables. Where there is insufficient space for a 2.1m (7-ft) table, a 1.8m (6-ft) table is ideal.

With the cushions, the playing surface is usually 0.3m (1 ft) less in length and width than the external measurement of the table.

Not all pool tables are covered with green cloth. Other colours are available to suit the décor of a particular location.

The cloth on a pool table is made from wool or nylon.

THE 'D' END

Traditionally, pool tables had a 'D' marked on the cloth. On modern tables the 'D' is now often replaced by a line right across the table (called the string line). This allows the player to break from anywhere behind the line.

Dusting the tip of the cue with chalk before you play ensures smooth contact with the cue ball and may prevent shots being miscued. Gently blow off any excess chalk.

BED MARKINGS

The cloth on the playing area bears certain markings (see diagram below). The 8-ball spot is located at the intersection of the diagonals of the central and bottom corner pockets. The 'string line' runs across the table, one-fifth of the distance from the top cushion to the bottom cushion. On the string line a 'D' is drawn towards the top cushion, the diameter of this is one-third of the width of the table. Some tables are marked with the string line right across the table. Tables with a marked string line can accommodate other games that can be played on pool tables.

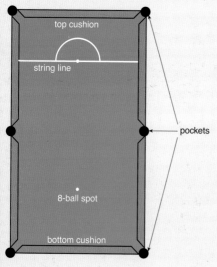

Table markings.

TABLE POSITIONING

The position of a pool table is important. Make sure there is enough room around the table to play a shot from every point with a standard size cue. (Very short cues are available to enable shots to be played from obstructed locations.) The table must be perfectly level. Tables should be placed in a permanent position, as moving the table may mean that it is no longer on the level.

MAINTAINING THE TABLE

A table needs to be maintained in good condition. The playing surface should be brushed daily with a soft nylon or horse hair brush, in the direction of the nap – from the 'D' to the bottom cushion. A cloth made of wool or wool/nylon should be ironed regularly, again in the direction of the nap. Before ironing, the cloth should be brushed and cleaned with a damp cloth to lift any surface grit and dirt. The pocket liners should be checked regularly to ensure that they are seated firmly in the pockets. It is also a good idea to check the shoes into which the balls drop and all other cosmetic fitments.

The torn cloth on this table renders it unfit for competition play.

Taking care to maintain the quality of the cloth on the table will ensure that it has a longer life span.

A piece of cloth can be used to rack up the balls. This prevents sweat being transmitted from your hands via the triangle on to the bed cloth.

PROTECTING THE CLOTH

It is important to look after the table by ensuring that it is clean and used in a careful manner. Players should always use cues that are in good condition. Never toss or drop coins on to the bed of the table – coins are the most common cause of small cuts appearing on the playing surface.

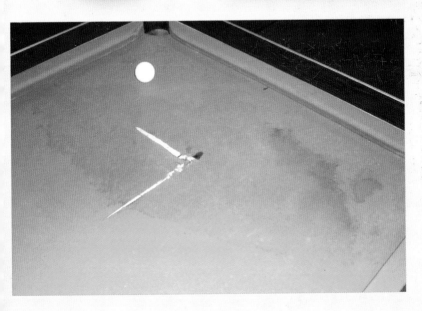

CUES

Pool cues are made of various woods, such as redwood, maple, willow, sandalwood and ash. Most cues supplied in licensed premises are a cheap softwood version imported from the Far East. These are normally 122cm (48 inches) long for a small table, and 137–145cm (54–57 inches) long for longer tables. The circumference at the handle end is roughly 9–10cm (3.5–4 inches).

Cues normally contain a metal weight at the thick end, and the tip is mounted in a metal or plastic ferrule. Cue tips are usually 11–12mm (0.43–0.47 inches) in diameter.

As the cues that are supplied with pool tables are for general use, they quickly become damaged. Always check the cue for sharp edges, particularly around the tip end. A ripped cloth can be a very expensive accident!

THE BALLS

The game of pool uses 16 balls. These are usually made of phenolic resin. All but the cue ball are usually 5.1cm (2 inches) in diameter. The cue ball is slightly smaller. It is plain white and is shared by both sides. The other balls, the object balls, are traditionally numbered 1 to 15. Number 8 (the '8-ball') is black, and the rest are coloured to divide them into two even groups.

Originally, numbers 1 to 7 were plain colours (known as the 'spots' or 'solids') and numbers 9 to 15 were striped (called the 'stripes'). However, the game is now commonly played with single coloured balls (seven red, seven yellow, one black and a white cue ball). Using unnumbered balls makes the lay of the balls easier to see and plan.

THE WARP FACTOR

Cues should always be stored in a cool, dry place. Storing them near radiators or in damp conditions may cause the wood to warp. To check if a cue is straight, roll it on the table. If it rolls evenly then it is still true, but if it jumps then something is wrong.

Keen players may choose to buy a higher quality hardwood cue of their own, with a smaller tip size of 8–10mm (0.31–0.39 inches) in diameter.

THE RACK

The rack is a triangle made of plastic or wood. It is used at the start of the game to place the balls in their correct positions.

The balls should be kept clean and smooth by an occasional polish with a soft rag.

This is the correct way to rack up the balls. The rack used here is for 8-ball rules pool.

This is the correct type of rack used for blackball rules pool.

Different types of cue and rest are available, along with specialist shorter cues.

LEARNING THE BASICS

The object of 8-ball pool is to use the white cue ball to knock your own seven balls into the pockets, then legally pot the black (the 8-ball). The skill is in learning to control the cue and predict where the balls will fall. For that, you first have to master the basics.

HOLDING THE CUE

Holding the cue correctly is mostly a question of comfort. Find the point of balance of the cue and grasp the cue lightly but securely a little behind this point (further towards you) with your strongest hand (the right, for right-handers). Trial and error will soon determine the most comfortable point of grip on any cue.

 Holding a cue for the first time can feel a little awkward to begin with.

THE BRIDGE

The tip end of the cue now needs a secure point on which to rest to ensure the tip makes smooth contact with the cue ball. For this, you need to master the bridge. The bridge is used to rest the cue on by the majority of players, with some minor personal touches.

Place the left hand (for right-handers) flat on the table, fingers pointing away from you. Leaving the heel of the hand on the table, draw the fingers back, bending them and leaving the tips touching the table.

 A player tests the point of balance of his cue.

Raise the thumb high, to form a 'V' between the thumb and forefinger knuckle, into which the shaft of the cue may be rested. Now bring the tips of the little finger and forefinger slightly behind the other two to create a firm base. This is a conventional bridge.

To form a raised bridge, raise the heel of the hand to make the cue strike the cue ball at a higher point. A raised bridge allows you to pass the cue over obstructing object balls.

BRIDGE CONTROL

The importance of the bridge is often underestimated. An otherwise excellent player will lose consistently through having a rickety bridge and mis-cueing relatively simple strokes.

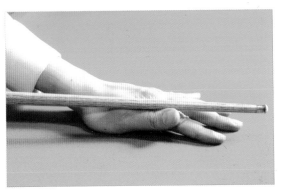

 A conventional bridge.

 A raised bridge.

In 8-ball or blackball pool, it does not matter in which order you pocket your seven balls – the numbers, if the balls have them, are irrelevant.

STANCE

To gain control over the cue, and over your game, you need to perfect your stance. Positioning your legs, body, arms and head in the right way will ensure that you have better vision and control over your shot. To practise the correct stance, first place one ball in the 'D' at the head of the table. Stand at a 45-degree angle to the table, with your bridge hand nearest the table, feet comfortably apart.

▼ The correct stance: see how the player has a direct line of sight along the cue to the cue ball.

Legs
With your feet in the same position, pivot round until you are facing the cue ball. Lean forwards to place the bridge hand in a position so that the cue will rest on it, with the tip almost touching and able to strike the cue ball.

Body
Keeping the near leg straight, bend forwards to bring the chin down until it almost touches the cue. Some players prefer to touch the cue lightly with the chin. This gives them a greater awareness of alignment with the cue ball.

STANCE

This is very much a question of personal comfort enabling the participant (player) to feel comfortable whilst holding the cue and addressing the ball. It is important that the stance is within the rules of the game as regards feet touching the floor – for example it is not acceptable to sit on the edge of the table. If it is difficult to address the ball then the player should use an appropriate rest.

Arms

You can now look forwards along the cue ball. Keep both eyes open. It is not like sighting a rifle over a long distance – the three-dimensional effect of both eyes provides a more accurate view. This will give you better alignment of cue and cue ball to ensure a smooth, straight, flowing movement. This is perhaps best achieved by locking the upper part of the cue arm into a position with the shoulder over the cue and the elbow in alignment with the shoulder, bridge hand and cue ball. Only the forearm is then allowed to move, swinging backwards and forwards in a smooth rhythm, carrying the cue straight towards its target. Many of the most accomplished players use this technique to avoid 'hooking' the cue arm.

◀ The player's body is at a slight angle to his legs.

▲ This player has his chin almost resting on the cue itself.

STRIKING THE CUE BALL

Before attempting shots at an object ball, practise with the cue ball only. Follow the steps below to practise striking the cue ball accurately.

1. Place the ball in the 'D' at the head of the table and take up your stance comfortably.

2. Sight along the cue, through the cue ball, to a position on the bottom cushion, exactly opposite the cue ball.

3. Make sure you are confident that you are moving the cue in a true line towards the centre of the cue ball and the target spot on the bottom cushion.

4. When you are satisfied, allow the cue to travel forwards to strike the cue ball.

5. Do not strike too hard. Try to judge the force of your strike so that the cue ball will return from the bottom cushion and come to rest at the tip of your waiting cue.

This is an excellent practice stroke and it will really help to improve the game of the player who can master it.

A practising player lines up a straight shot at the cue ball, aiming for the centre of the bottom cushion.

The more you practise with the cue ball, the more in control of your game you will be.

CONTROL OF THE CUE BALL

Control of the cue ball, both before and after striking the target, is the most important of the many skills required to make a good player. This skill is the one which ensures that you consistently win.

For the beginner and the competent player, working on the precise control of the cue ball is one of the most important skills to practise.

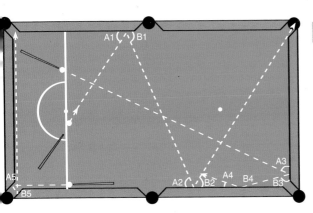

Angles of shots played full ball against the cushion.

CUSHIONS

At first, many beginners have difficulty working out the angles of shots played against the cushion. It may help to think of it in the following manner. If a tennis ball is dropped on to a flat surface, it will bounce back in a straight line. However, should it be thrown at a slight angle it will bounce away at

an angle equal to that at which it approached the ground. A pool ball reacts in exactly the same manner when striking the cushion of the table (see diagram above). Unless 'side' has been put on to the ball (see page 19), angles A and B will always be equal. The ability to 'play all the angles' accurately is essential.

CHECK AND SIDE

The way you strike the cue ball will determine what happens when it contacts an object ball or cushion. You can apply check, follow through or side to a cue ball to affect the impact it has on an object ball.

1. Applying check
By striking the cue ball below the centre line you can increase the degree of 'check' on its progress when it strikes an object ball. The lower the strike, the greater the check. When hit at its lowest point, the cue ball will hit the object ball and 'screw back' (return along the cue-line). A screw back shot may enable you to pot a straight ball into the pocket without following it in with the cue ball, and thus prevent a foul stroke ('in off' see pages 26).

2. Applying follow through
If the cue ball is struck above the centre line the degree of check is decreased on impact and it will increasingly tend to 'follow through' according to how high it has been struck.

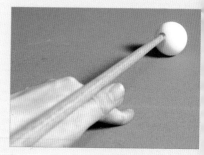

To apply follow through, strike the cue ball above the centre line (looking down the cue).

To apply check, strike the cue ball below the centre line (looking down the cue).

These strikes can be combined to produce right-hand check or follow-through, and left-hand check or follow-through.

3. Applying left- and right-hand side

The cue ball can also be steered after it strikes an object ball. If it is struck to the left of the centre it will run to the left. If struck to the right of centre the ball will run to the right. This is referred to as putting 'side' on the cue ball. This stroke is sometimes useful to change the angle of the cue ball as it returns from the cushion.

PRACTICE MAKES PERFECT

The degree to which all these things are varied can vastly change the action of the cue ball. Practising the way you strike the cue ball is vital. Only experimentation will determine what you personally can achieve.

To apply left-hand side, strike the cue ball to the left of the centre line (looking down the cue).

To apply right-hand side, strike the cue ball to the right of the centre line (looking down the cue).

Here, the player has a difficult angle to contend with.

Swerve: spin is applied to the cue ball to project it around the obstructing ball.

POTTING

There are several points to consider before attempting to pot a ball: direction of the cue ball, momentum of the object ball, and position of the cue ball.

Direction

To pot an object ball, it is important to ensure that the cue ball strikes it at the correct point.

- For a straight shot, this should be the centre.

- When cutting the ball into a pocket to the left of the line from the cue ball to object ball, the object ball should be struck on the right.

- When cutting the ball into a pocket to the right of the line from the cue to the object ball, strike the object ball on the left.

 This player's shot is right on target.

Momentum

When the cue ball strikes an object ball, it gives the object ball momentum.

- The nearer to the centre of the object ball that the cue ball strikes, the greater the momentum it will gain and the less acute the angle of travel will be.

- The nearer the outside the object ball is struck by the cue ball, the less momentum is transferred and the wider the angle of travel.

An object ball struck full face will travel at almost the same speed as the striking cue ball, while an object ball struck on the extreme edge will gain very little momentum.

CAREFULLY DOES IT

The more accurately you need to strike the object ball, the more careful you need to be in assessing the force required. Many players will use unnecessary force, incurring penalties that could have been avoided with practice and planning.

 A player aims to pot an object ball with a straight shot.

Cue-ball position

The cue ball bounces from the object ball in a very similar manner to that in which it bounces from the cushion apart from the momentum it loses. Always consider the direction the cue ball will take after striking the object ball. Ensure that it goes where you want it, so that it works to your advantage, not your opponent's.

This player is aiming to leave the cue ball in a place that will obstruct his opponent.

A player attempts to pot an object ball using the cue ball to strike it from the side.

Remember: control that cue ball.

PLAYING THE GAME

Pool is a social game of skill, full of drama, glorious shots and near misses. This section of the book focuses on the opening of the game, issues that may come up during play, such as snookers, fouls and penalties, and of course, how the game is won.

NOTE ON THE RULES

The rules for 8-ball pool, which can be found in full on pages 48-53, are quite brief and were carefully written by BAPTO in 1975. (You can find the rules for blackball pool on pages 54–55.) Modifications to the rules have been made since then with the aim of making the game as fair as possible and to alter rules that unscrupulous players have abused. Players often discuss exactly what is meant by particular rules, and points not mentioned in the rules. The explanation of the game that follows should help with some of these problems.

> Players or teams should always agree on what is fair before play begins.

DISPUTES

It is important to any competition or league to rule that if a match is played or continued after a dispute, any irregularity will be deemed to have been accepted. The result will then stand by the referee's decision with no possibilities of appeal.

TERMINOLOGY

The following terms will come up in this section of the book and are explained below.

- **Break** First shot of the game or first shot of a re-started game.

- **Shot** Striking the cue ball once.

- **Visit** One turn at the table comprising one or a series of shots.

RACKING

The first step in the game is to place the balls on the table. A rack in the form of a solid triangle is used to place the balls accurately. The black ball is placed on the 8-ball spot marked on the table. This is at the intersection of the centre and bottom corner pockets.

The triangle fans out towards the bottom cushion with the head (single) ball facing the 'D'. Balls of different combination are placed at the corners. When the object balls have been placed, the 8-ball should be sitting in the centre of the third row.

 A player racks up the object balls and the 8-ball (black).

This player has just made the first break.

STARTING THE GAME

Traditionally, the order of play is decided by tossing a coin. The winner of the toss can choose to make the first shot (break), or ask his or her opponent to do so. Alternatively, players may lag as in blackball rules.

MAKING A BREAK

The opening player places the cue ball at any point on or within the 'D', and plays it into the triangle of object balls. The break must be sufficient to either pocket a ball or cause at least two balls to return to the half of the table containing the 'D'. If the player does not manage this, a foul break has occurred. In the event of a foul break, the balls are re-racked and the opposing player re-starts the game with one shot plus one visit. The offending player loses a turn at the table.

NOTES ON BREAK SHOTS

Whether or not a ball is potted from a legal break, the breaking-player must nominate his or her choice of object balls.

- If no balls are pocketed from the break, the breaking player must nominate his or her choice and continue to play on the nominated group. Any illegally pocketed ball is ignored in determining which group the players are on.

A player prepares to make a break.

- If a foul shot is committed at the break and one or more object balls pocketed, those balls are ignored in determining the groups to be played. The next player may then play at any ball on the table (except the 8-ball). The breaking player, however, would still have nominated his or her choice of group of object balls. This rule applies only to the break (first) shot.

- If a player pockets the 8-ball from the break, the game is re-started by the same player. This applies only on the break shot.

- When a player legally pockets a ball or balls, he or she will continue by playing another shot. This carries on until the player either fails to pocket one of his or her object balls or commits a foul.

SNOOKERED!

A player is snookered when there is no 'full ball shot' at any of his or her balls. This means that, looking in a straight line from behind the cue ball to the object ball in question, the player cannot see the whole circumference of the object ball (the centre of the object ball cannot be struck by the centre of the cue ball). It does not matter whether one of the sides can be played and, in this respect, pool differs from the game of snooker.

COMBINATION SHOTS

When the cue ball hits an object ball that then hits another object ball, it is known as a combination shot. Combinations are allowed provided the player hits one of his or her own object balls first. Following a foul, a player may, on the first shot only, hit any ball on the table (see Rule 6, pages 50–51).

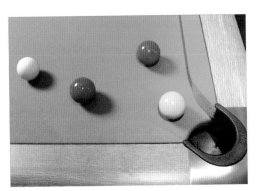

A snooker: there is no full ball shot to pot the object ball into the pocket.

Identifying a snooker.

A snookered ball can be played off a cushion.

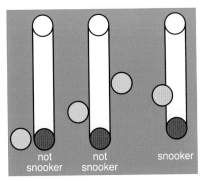

not snooker   not snooker   snooker

FOULS

When a foul is committed, the oncoming player is awarded an extra shot. It is a foul when any of the following occurs:

- The white cue ball is pocketed. This is known as 'in off'. If this occurs, the cue ball is replaced at any position on or within the 'D'.

- The cue ball strikes the opponent's ball before the player's own ball or balls.

- A player fails to hit any ball with the cue ball.

- The cue ball jumps over any part of any ball by accident or design before hitting any ball at all. This is known as a 'jump shot'.

- The cue ball hits the 8-ball (black) on the first impact before all the player's own balls have been pocketed (except where Rule 6(b) applies – see pages 50–51).

- A player pots his or her opponent's ball (unless on a combination shot when the player hits their own ball first, potting both one of his own and an

A ball is deemed to be off the table if it stops anywhere other than on the bed of the table.

opponents ball on the same shot or on the free shot following a foul).

- A ball goes off the table. Object balls should be placed on the 8-ball spot or as near as possible to the 8-ball spot in a direct line between the head spot and the centre of the 'D'.

- A player does not have at least one foot on the floor.

- A player strikes with the cue any ball other than the cue ball.

- A player plays out of turn.

- A player plays before all balls have come to rest.

- A player plays before the ball or balls have been re-spotted (replaced in the appropriate places).

- A player's clothing or body touches any ball.

- A player interferes with the movement of the ball with body, clothing or cue.

- A player strikes the cue ball with the cue more than once.

- A player plays a push shot, whereby the cue stays in contact as the cue ball rolls.

A foul is committed if a player does not have at least one foot on the floor.

Even if the ball does not move when part of the player or their clothing touches it, a foul should be called.

A foul is committed if a player strikes with the cue any ball other than the cue ball.

A player commits a foul if part of their clothing touches a ball.

PENALTY FOR A FOUL

The penalty for a foul is for a player to concede one extra shot to his or her opponent. The oncoming player has one free shot, whether an object ball is potted or not, before playing their due turn.

When a foul shot occurs, the offended player must claim his or her free shot immediately. If the offending player is allowed to continue without challenge, the opportunity of a free shot is lost.

AFTER A FOUL

Following any foul, the oncoming player, for the first shot of his first visit only, is free to play at any ball without nomination and without penalty. This includes the opponent's ball and the 8-ball (black), whether or not the player is snookered. All balls potted directly or by combination are considered legally potted (except the 8-ball, which would lose him the game).

After any foul stroke, the offended player may play the ball from where it lies or from any position within the 'D'.

FOUL PLAY

Formerly, the penalty for a foul was for a player to lose his or her next visit to the table. However, since the introduction of the cue ball in-hand whereby the offended player may move the cue ball to anywhere within the 'D', that penalty has been considered too severe.

 An offended player claims his entitlement for a foul.

A referee may advise on rules if asked, otherwise he will simply administer the rules of the game.

An offended player places the cue ball on the 'D'. Moving the ball in this way does not count as a shot or visit.

WINNING THE GAME

After potting all seven object balls, a player has to pot the 8-ball (black) to win the game. It is not necessary to nominate the pocket in which the black (or any other ball) is potted.

If a player pots the 8-ball and any other ball on the same stroke they will lose the game. However, following a foul when only the 8-ball and one or more balls of the opponent's group are left, the player may legally pot the 8-ball and others in any order.

DRAWN GAME

In the event where a legal shot cannot be played, the game is re-started, whether the situation has arisen by accident or design.

STALEMATE

In any pool competition a referee should be appointed. If it seems that both players intend to play a continuous sequence of non-potting safe shots (trying to place the ball, so your opponent will struggle to play the next shot), the referee may intervene. The referee may enforce a re-start if the position remains in stalemate after the next visit to the table by both players.

A player prepares to take the winning shot.

29

STRATEGY

Pool differs substantially from snooker and billiards in playing strategy, as many an old hand at snooker has discovered with embarrassment. In snooker and billiards, few if any balls are denied to a player, provided he or she has followed the correct sequence. In pool, however, a player may not play or pot seven balls plus the black, from almost the commencement of the game, without incurring penalties or overcoming several very tricky shots.

COVERING POCKETS

A player can 'cover' the pockets of the table. By placing object balls of his or her own group in a position near a pocket, the player can effectively deny the use of that pocket to the opponent. Accomplished players often take a more difficult shot, rather than sink a ball sitting over a pocket. The 'sitter' makes it difficult for the opponent to progress.

OBSTRUCTING YOUR OPPONENT

You must always bear in mind that your objective is not only to pot your own balls, but also to ensure that you prevent your opponent potting theirs. Two useful tactics that will do much to improve your own chances of success are:

- obstruct your opponent's play with your own object balls

- place the cue ball in positions to cause your opponent the greatest difficulty.

Remember, however, that you cannot win a game without potting balls, and playing in an over-cautious manner can often benefit your opponent more than yourself.

This player is tactically taking a more difficult shot in order to leave one of his object balls covering the middle pocket.

RELAX!

One final word of advice is to relax. Pool is not a game that can be played well in a hurry. You will never be likely to win any game by a rushed and ill-considered approach. Before you even pick up your cue remember to:

- slow down

- concentrate on what you wish to achieve and put other thoughts out of your head

- think about how you will play to win.

By doing this you will give yourself that extra 'edge' that wins matches.

A good player does not always sink the ball played towards a pocket. The ball is of more value left on the table until he or she can pot all seven object balls followed by the 8-ball (black).

The cue ball's position will make it difficult for the oncoming player to make a clean shot.

It is important to feel relaxed and in a calm, focused frame of mind before playing each shot.

COMPETITION ORGANISATION

Pool can be an exciting game, where opponents use their skill and clever tactics to try and outplay each other. Friendly matches are a great way of socialising with friends and pitting your wits against them. League or knockout competitions add challenge and incentive to the mix.

PREPARATION

Before discussing the mechanics of organising competitions, it is important to consider the interests of everyone concerned:

- the landlord, manager or owner of the premises
- the pool players
- non-pool playing users of the premises.

Pub landlords have to strike a delicate balance: increasing their business by keeping the pool players happy, without alienating other customers who may resent an invasion of their privacy by players and spectators from elsewhere.

> **Always include the landlord in discussions to do with staging a competition.**

LEAGUES

The first step in setting up a league is to establish the degree of interest. This will usually take the form of a letter of invitation containing outline proposals, including such matters as:

- area in which the league is to operate
- length of season
- match nights and starting times
- rules
- constitution – conditions to supplement the rules (see pages 52–53)
- sponsorships or other prizes
- number of teams per location
- number of players/registrations (for example six players registered to ensure there is always a team of four available, and 12 registered for a team of eight)

- number of teams per league
- pool table specifications
- registration fees
- committees
- Referees.

The procedure outlined above applies to area knockout competitions. For individual house competitions most of the formalities may be dispensed with.

LAUNCHING A COMPETITION

Once there is sufficient response, the next step is to decide on the type and amount of advertising and other supporting literature required to launch the competition. This can prove costly (unless sponsorship is available). The alternative is to use one's own resources as much as possible. However, be wary of 'cheap and nasty' visuals, particularly posters, which may appear unprofessional.

ESSENTIAL ITEMS

In order to set up a league, the following items are essential and are covered in full on pages 34–39:

- posters
- registration forms
- results sheets
- fixture lists
- rules and constitution
- timetable
- publicity.

Winners of a tournament proudly accept their hard won trophies.

POSTERS

If you are planning a competition, make sure you produce an eye-catching poster to announce details such as the date, time and location, the prizes available and how to enter. Match posters may also attract spectators, which will increase business on the night.

REGISTRATION FORMS

If your budget allows, producing printed team or individual cards with photographs of players adds a touch of professionalism. With access to a computer, you could simply compile and print these yourself to cut costs.

The forms should be distributed with posters, and authenticated before the first matches are due to be played.

REGISTRATION CARD				
TEAM NAME & ADDRESS			Tel.	
	Name	Signature	Name	Signature
1			7	
2			8	
3			9	
4			10	
5			11	
6			12	

Name and Signature of Landlord _____ DATE

A registration card.

RESULT CARD			
Home Team		Away Team	
	Home		Away
	Name	Signature	Name	Signature
1			
2			
3			
4			
5			
6			
7			
8			
9			

Date _____ Comp t n/Div _____ Home Score _____ Away Score _____
Home _____ Away Captain _____

A result card.

RESULTS SHEETS

Results sheets may be produced locally, but a pre-paid postcard will help to ensure speedy reporting of match results. Alternatively results may be notified by phone or e-mail.

An eyecatching poster will attract competitors and spectators.

When playing as a team, it is important to recognise strengths and weaknesses in other team members as this will affect your playing strategy.

Registration cards should be prepared in duplicate. One copy is kept by the organisers and the other is stamped and returned to the team for production at matches.

AUTHENTICATION

Registration is often subject to abuse. Competition organisers are well advised to ensure that only registered players represent a particular team. A reasonably accurate system is to crosscheck names and signatures on result cards with those on the organiser's copy of registration forms.

FIXTURE LISTS

There may be two separate types of fixture list. It is important to publish one list for the full season. This may also be supplemented by monthly fixture lists, to clarify the situation. An example of a fixture list is shown below.

Each team should be scheduled to play each other team in the league once away and once at home each season. Compiling fixture lists can be a mathematician's nightmare, particularly if there are houses with two teams in divisions with different numbers of teams!

Pre-plan dates for all competitions being organised. In the fixture list shown below a clear date has been reserved for knockout competitions at the stage where all teams are involved. You will also see that certain numbers in the fixture formula are 'paired', for example teams 2 and 7 are never 'at home' on the same day, so these pairings are used for locations with two teams but only one pool table.

> **Always attempt to write fixtures in each division for the same number of teams.**

> **Always ensure that houses with two teams avoid a clash of home venue. This is easier to achieve when each division in an organised league has the same number of teams.**

An example of a fixture list for a pool tournament.

Fixtures for the Joe Bloggs Bloggsville & District League
The following fixtures apply to all divisions except 'D' division

Oct 3	Oct 10	Oct 17	Oct 24	Oct 31	Nov 7	Nov 14	Nov 21	Nov 28	Dec 5	Dec 12
2v1	1v3	4v1	1v5	Team KO		6v1	1v7	8v1	1v9	10v1
3v9	10v2	3v2	2v4	7 Man		5v2	2v6	7v2	2v8	9v2
4v8	9v4	5v9	10v3	Home & Away		4v3	3v5	6v3	3v7	8v3
5v7	8v5	6v8	9v6	Aggregate		7v9	10v4	5v4	4v6	7v4
6v10	7v6	7v10	8v7	will count		8v10	9v8	9v10	10v5	6v5
Jan 9	Jan 16	Jan 23	Jan 30			Feb 20	Feb 27	Mar 6	Mar 13	Mar 20

Singles first round will be on December 19; 3-team KO Feb 6 & 13.

The following fixtures apply to 'D' division. Note the four Wednesday matches

Oct 3	Oct 10	Oct 17	Oct 24	Wed Nov 2	Wed Nov 9	Nov 14	Nov 21	Nov 28	Dec 5	Dec 12
2v1	1v3	4v1	1v5	12v1	1v11	6v1	1v7	8v1	1v9	10v1
3v11	12v2	3v2	2v4	2v10	11v2	5v2	2v6	7v2	2v8	9v2
4v10	11v4	5v11	12v3	3v9	10v3	4v3	3v5	6v3	3v7	8v3
5v9	10v5	6v10	11v6	4v8	9v4	7v11	12v4	5v4	4v6	7v4
6v8	9v6	7v9	10v7	5v7	8v5	8v10	11v8	9v11	12v5	6v5
7v12	8v7	8v12	9v8	6v12	7v6	9v12	10v9	10v12	11v10	11v12
Jan 9	Jan 16	Jan 23	Jan 30	Feb 1	Feb 15	Feb 20	Feb 27	Mar 6	Mar 13	Mar 20

RULES AND CONSTITUTION

Playing to a standard of rules enables players across the league and in different venues to be consistent with one another. A rules chart should be prominently displayed wherever pool is played. In addition to the basic rules for 8-ball pool, there will be conditions and procedures which are appropriate to that particular competition. These should be prominently displayed or readily available on match nights.

Providing players and officials with pocket-sized cards containing the rules, the constitution and notes for the guidance of referees adds a little extra polish to the proceedings.

FLAG UP UNUSUAL POINTS

It is always desirable to draw attention to anything out of the ordinary on a fixture list, for example if there are some fixtures scheduled for an alternative day to the rest of the fixtures.

In particular try to cover any issues which have previously caused a problem.

The official BAPTO rules appear on pages 48–53.

Players shake hands before playing in a competition.

TIMETABLE

Effective planning and organisation are key to ensuring that a tournament runs smoothly. To help with the planning you may find it useful to produce something along the lines of the specimen 'critical path analysis' shown below. The example used here shows that not all the literature is required at once and that more than one activity can be planned to take place simultaneously.

By keeping a timetable of events the organisers should be able to issue the competition kit about two weeks before the first matches are due to be played.

Large committees may become too unwieldy to be effective and should be avoided at all costs.

 This match is being televised.

 Example of a critical path analysis for pool.

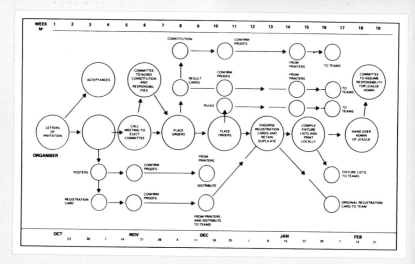

Once orders for the paperwork have been placed, the organisers must decide how the league is to be run, either by themselves, a representative committee, or the sponsors. A meeting should then be arranged as soon as possible. Whichever method is adopted, the organisers need to delegate responsibilities and establish procedures for dealing with situations that may arise, such as disputes.

PUBLICITY

Try to get as much local press coverage as possible. Most local papers will be happy to publish league results and tables on a regular basis.

When it comes to organising competitions, it can sometimes feel like you are buried under a mountain of thankless tasks. There will even be times when you wonder why you ever bothered. Don't lose heart. As long as your planning is good and your administration sound, the only criticisms you will hear will be those of the bad losers – and they don't count.

BASIC COMPETITION KIT

The basic competition kit usually contains the following items:

- endorsed registration cards
- sufficient result cards for half a season
- rules card
- constitution
- match posters and individual pocket cards, if available.

Midway through the competition, posters and rule cards should be replaced by fresh material and the second batch of result cards. It is a good idea to retain a small number of all supporting literature and promotional material in case replacements are needed.

'A' Division	'B' Division	'C' Division
(1) Talbot 'C'	(1) Talbot 'A'	(1) Black Bull 'B'
(2) Brunshaw 'B'	(2) Bridge 'A'	(2) Gen. Havelock 'A'
(3) Station (Nelson)	(3) Dragoon 'B'	(3) Griffin 'A'
(4) Corporation 'A'	(4) Wellington	(4) Woodman 'A'
(5) Gannow Wharf 'A'	(5) Rose & Crown	(5) Old Duke
(6) Black Bull 'A'	(6) Talbot 'B'	(6) Rifle Vols 'B'
(7) Brunshaw 'A'	(7) Briercliffe W.M.C.	(7) Gen. Havelock 'B'
(8) Dragoon 'A'	(8) Bay Horse	(8) Town Mouse 'A'
(9) Corporation 'C'	(9) Waggoners 'A'	(9) Corporation 'B'
(10) Frames	(10) Dugdale	(10) Mitre

'D' Division	'E' Division	'F' Division
(1) Adelphi	(1) Fighting Cocks 'B'	(1) Cattle Market
(2) Alma	(2) Carlton W.M.C.	(2) Bridge 'C'
(3) Borough	(3) Griffin 'B'	(3) Town Mouse 'B'
(4) Brickmakers 'A'	(4) Royal Butterfly	(4) Waggoners 'B'
(5) Marsden Cross	(5) Concert Artists 'A'	(5) Louie's 'B'
(6) Old Bridge	(6) Nelson	(6) Talbot 'D'
(7) Fighting Cocks 'A'	(7) Coach & Horses	(7) Rose & Thistle
(8) Bridge 'B'	(8) Feathers	(8) Dragoon 'C'
(9) Oxford	(9) Gordon Lennox	(9) Woodman 'B'
(10) Brickmakers 'B'	(10) Gannow Wharf 'B'	(10) Concert Artists 'B'
(11) Louie's 'A'		
(12) Rifle Vols 'A'		

 Team classifications.

TOURNAMENTS

A well-run tournament provides fair and sporting competition as opposed to confrontation. The players themselves will usually lift their game to fit the occasion.

Tournaments may be team or individual affairs and usually concern the winners of some earlier rounds or minor competitions. It is essential that the number of contestants can be accommodated within the available resources of finance, equipment, manpower, time and space.

PLANNING

Advertising the tournament on the basis of bigger prizes will attract more entrants in the initial stages of the competition. Make sure that money has been set aside for hiring the venue, audio, lighting and other equipment, and to pay for officials, promotional literature and other basic requirements.

NUMBER OF MATCHES

The time available for the tournament should be calculated along with the number of tables required. A simple and useful formula can be used for all knockout competitions: the number of matches to be played is always one less than the number of competitors. For example, four competitors: two semi-finals, plus one final = three games; 119 competitors involves 55 preliminary matches and nine byes to reduce to 64 entrants; 32 first round matches followed in subsequent rounds by 16, eight, four and two culminating in one final match to total 118.

In considering a budget for the event, there is more incentive if fewer people compete for bigger prizes rather than staging a large competition with smaller prizes.

NUMBER OF GAMES

The maximum number of games required is calculated on the basis of whatever criteria constitute a match (for example one game only or best of three). Singles will normally take not more than 15 minutes. Roughly 20 minutes should usually be sufficient for doubles. A time limit may be stipulated for games if necessary.

ENSURING FAIRNESS

Apart from special equipment, the pool tables should be chosen carefully. This is to ensure that, as far as possible, no player can be deemed to have any advantage over another.

Avoiding overcrowding ensures that players have a calm, safe environment in which to enjoy the game.

NUMBER OF TABLES

Once you know how many games are required you can calculate the number of tables and time required to complete a particular programme. Avoid overcrowding at all costs, as jostling among players or spectators is likely to spoil the game and cause chaos. The landlord of the venue will probably be able to advise on health and safety issues.

In allocating order for play, the organisers should ensure that all pool tables are fully utilised, even if it means having more than one stage or competition running simultaneously.

TYPES OF TOURNAMENT

Tournaments can take many forms. The most common formats are listed below.

1. Straight run knockout competition
A given number of contestants is gradually reduced to an outright winner on an eliminator basis. This is simple and easy to run.

2. Double elimination knockout competition
First time losers have an opportunity to stay in the competition by being drawn against other losers. This can be complicated and time-consuming.

3. Grouping Contestants are grouped as in the soccer World Cup, followed by a knockout competition between group winners. This format is popular with players, as they stay in the competition for longer.

TIPS FOR SUCCESS

Whatever method you choose, keep everyone informed of what is going on at every stage of the tournament. Clear visual aids can be a great asset here.

Possibly the best investment of all lies in the employment of officials: polite and efficient staff help the event to run smoothly. When hiring tournament officials, it is worth remembering the following points:

- professional referees have presence and can command respect from players and spectators alike

- clear and concise announcements on a good public address system assist the smooth flow of each stage of the competition

- efficient and courteous service at the bar and food counters make spectators feel welcome and respected

- capable door attendants can ensure that gatecrashers are refused admission.

In larger venues, several matches can be played at the same time. This helps keep the tournament within a shorter time frame.

In the interests of fair play, make sure that winning players are not allocated the same table throughout the competition.

GOLDEN RULES

Remember the following golden rules and you will be well on the way to organising a successful pool tournament.

1. Make sure money and prizes are available as advertised.

2. Do not try to achieve too much in the time available.

3. Select the best possible premises in terms of space.

4. Use only first-class tables and equipment.

5. Employ efficient and courteous officials.

6. Get your sums right.

7. Keep everyone informed of what is happening.

8. Avoid overcrowding.

NOTES FOR REFEREES

The referee of a pool match has an important role to play. The referee is there to ensure fairness throughout the game and to provide guidance to the players should they need it during a game. It is the referee's job to administer the rules and ensure they are properly followed. The referee has the power to abandon or postpone a game, and also to disqualify a player. As with all sports, the referee's decision is final.

REF'S RESPONSIBILITIES

The full list of the referee's responsibilities is outlined below.

1. It is important that the referee understands the game rules and he must be assured that the players also have read and understood the same rules.

2. The referee must also have read and understood the rules governing the procedure of that competition or league and must be assured that the players have also read and understood the same rules.

3. The referee shall determine the conduct for the match in progress and is empowered to abandon, postpone or disqualify.

4. Careful thought must be given before deciding on a course of drastic action as in note 3. It is advisable to suspend play and then talk to the two players or two captains before making a final decision. The referee should suspend play immediately, obtain the facts, then make a decision.

5. It is advisable to draw the two captains aside before the game starts and briefly run over certain points that are often not widely understood. The referee should make quite clear what interpretation he or she will make in certain circumstances, for example:

(a) Following a foul, the oncoming (offended) player is granted a free shot in which to play the ball from where it lies or from within the 'D', and may play any ball, but must not pot the black. Following this free single shot, the player's visit to the table commences.

(b) The cue ball may be played in any direction from within the 'D', which is also described as 'cue ball in-hand'.

(c) Player in control rule – vibration pot (see note 16 on page 46 and box on page 47).

(d) The referee should clarify what

happens if a player is unable or unwilling to complete the game.

6. Before the beginning of the game the referee must ensure that the balls are correctly racked, with the 8-ball (black) in the centre of the third row on the spot at the intersection of the centre and bottom pockets, the others alternating high and low wherever possible. This method of racking the balls has proven to produce the fairest spread of object balls following the break.

7. The referee should ensure that both captains understand what situations may result in the loss of a game:

(a) Illegal potting of the 8-ball (see Rules 7(a), (b) and (c) on page 51).

(b) Cue or any object ball in off the 8-ball when the 8-ball is legally potted.

8. If a player deliberately alters the course of a ball or obstructs a pocket opening, a foul shall be awarded.

REFEREE'S RULING

Abandonment means a NIL result for both parties. Postponement allows a second chance to establish a result. In certain circumstances this can be done immediately by re-starting a game. Disqualification of one or other of the parties gives the game to the other.

The referee must keep a close eye on proceedings to ensure fair play.

In an official competition it is not usual for a player to rack up the balls.

9. If anyone other than the two players interferes with the playing of the game, then the referee at that time can choose the option of either having the balls replaced in their original positions and the shot replayed, or re-starting the game.

10. In the event of a player or players being considered incapable of offering fair and just competition because of either drink or drugs, the referee should be prepared to warn initially.

11. Dependent on the rules of that particular competition or league, a substitute may be allowed, providing that the player satisfies registration conditions.

12. If a player is deliberately coached by any other player or spectator, then the referee, at his discretion, may warn that further occurrences will cause the game to be abandoned, or awarded at his discretion.

13. The referee shall call all fouls and penalties and will make it clear to the players when they have to cease playing.

14. In the event of a player being about to play an obvious foul stroke the referee shall not warn him before the stroke is taken (see note 17).

15. The referee shall not advise or warn a player before a stroke. He may give a ruling if approached by a player before taking his shot.

16. In the event of a ball being accidentally vibrated into a pocket then the player in control rule shall apply (see 'In Control' box opposite).

17. The referee shall ensure that both players are clear on which group of object balls they are playing for. This is particularly important where a player has potted one or more of either set and is taking a choice.

18. The referee should take particular care when a player is playing away from a touching ball or aiming a shot that could produce a foul shot by the player not striking his own set of object balls first.

19. The referee should take particular care when a player is making a high bridge over his own or opponent's balls, and take particular note of the cuff of the sleeve if a coat is being worn by the player.

20. To miscue a ball shall not be a foul in itself. A foul may only be called on the result of the stroke.

21. The referee may not wager or accept any remuneration on the result of a game.

22. The referee shall ensure that the scorecard is properly marked and signed by officials according to the rules of the league or competition in which they are entered.

'IN CONTROL'

A player is deemed to be 'in control' from the time that any part of him or her, including clothing and cue, touches the table prior to a shot, through the visit and until such time as his or her opponent touches the table.

If competition is unrealistic, play should be suspended, but the referee should try to arrive at an amicable solution before making his final decision.

A competition referee ensures the balls are racked up correctly at the start of a match.

RULES OF 8-BALL POOL

The most popular pool game in the UK is 8-ball pool. This section of the book contains the rules as set out by BAPTO. In order to avoid time-consuming and heated debate during a match, it is important that both players or teams and the referee have read and understood the rules of the game before play commences.

1. THE GAME

The game shall be known as 8-ball pool and referred to in these rules as 'the game'. It is intended that players and teams should play 8-ball pool in the true spirit of the game and in a sporting manner. It should be clearly understood that the referee is the sole judge of what is fair and unfair play. The referee will take whatever action is necessary to ensure that these rules are observed.

2. REQUIREMENTS OF THE GAME

The game is played on a rectangular six-pocket table with 15 balls, plus a cue ball. Balls comprise two groups, represented by two different coloured balls plus the 8-ball, which is black. Balls in two groups are known as object balls.

Alternatively, numerical balls may be used, numbered 1 to 7, which are plain coloured balls, and 9 to 15, which are striped coloured balls.

3. OBJECT OF THE GAME

The player or team pocketing their group of object balls first in any order and then legally pocketing the 8-ball (black), wins the game.

4. COMMENCEMENT (OR RE-START) OF THE GAME

The opening of the game involves the break and nomination of the balls as follows.

(a) The balls are racked as illustrated here with the 8-ball (black) on the 8-ball spot, which is at the intersection of the centre and corner pockets.

Once this player has made the first break he can then nominate his set of object balls.

Traditional object balls are 'spots' and 'stripes'.

(b) Order of play is determined by the flip of a coin. The winner of the flip has the option of breaking or requesting his or her opponent to do so.

(c) The opening player plays at the triangle of object balls by striking the cue balls from any position on or within the 'D'. That player must pot one or more object balls or cause at least two object balls to return to an imaginary line joining the two centre pockets, i.e. to the 'D' half of the table. This constitutes a legal break. The breaking player shall then verbally nominate his or her group of object balls before play continues, even if a foul has been committed (except as in 4(f)).

(d) Any balls potted prior to groups being nominated are ignored for the purpose of establishing a player's group of object balls.

(e) If a legal break has not been achieved (except as in 4(f)) the breaking player shall nominate his or her object ball group before the oncoming player continues as described in 6(b).

(f) If the player pockets the 8-ball (black) from the break, the game shall be re-started by the same player. No penalty will be incurred, and the balls are re-racked. This applies even if other balls, including the cue ball, are pocketed as well.

(g) If a ball or balls are legally pocketed, this entitles the player to one additional shot and this continues until the player either:

(i) fails to pocket one of his or her set of allocated balls, or

(ii) commits a foul, at any time.

(h) Combination shots are allowed provided that the player hits one of his or her own group of balls first (unless Rule 6(b) applies).

(i) A player may legally pocket one or more of his or her opponent's object balls providing the cue ball strikes one of his or her own group first and providing one or more of his or her own group are pocketed on the same shot.

5. FOULS

The following is a list of fouls, for which the penalty is a free shot to the offended player.

(a) In off (cue ball pocketed).

(b) Hitting opponent's balls before one's own ball or balls, except when Rule 6(b) applies.

(c) Failing to hit any ball with the cue ball.

(d) Jump shots (cue ball jumping over any part of any ball before making contact with any object ball).

(e) Hitting the 8-ball (black) with the cue ball on the first impact before one's own balls have been potted, except when Rule 6(b) applies.

(f) Potting any opponent's balls except when Rule 4(i) or 6(b) applies.

(g) Ball off the table:

(i) Any object ball or the 8-ball (black) shall be returned to the 8-ball spot (see 4(a)) or as near as possible to that spot without touching any other ball, in a direct line between the spot and the centre of the 'D'.

(ii) If the cue ball, it is to be played from any position on or within the 'D'. A ball shall be deemed to be 'off the table' if it comes to rest other than on the bed of the table.

(h) If a player's clothing or body should touch any ball.

(i) Player not having at least one foot on the floor.

(j) Playing or touching with the cue any ball other than the cue ball.

(k) Playing out of turn.

(l) Playing before balls have come to rest.

(m) Playing before the ball or balls have been re-spotted.

(n) Striking the cue ball with any part of the cue other than the tip.

(o) Striking the cue ball with the cue more than once.

(p) Playing a shot before the breaking player has nominated a group of object balls following the break shot.

(q) Failing to achieve a legal break as described in Rule 4(c).

(r) Push stroke (see 8(a) on page 52).

(s) Moving an object ball or the 8-ball (black) when playing away from a touching ball.

6. PENALTY FOLLOWING A FOUL

Penalties for any foul are as follows.

(a) Following a foul, the oncoming player may play the cue ball from where it lies or from the 'D' (as in Rule 8(b)) and proceed as 6(b). Moving the cue ball to the 'D' does not constitute a shot or visit.

(b) Following a foul, the oncoming player is entitled to one free shot with which he or she may, without nomination, play the cue ball directly on to any ball, including opponent's object balls and the 8-ball (black). However, the oncoming player may not pocket the 8-ball (black), which would mean loss of the game, unless the player has already pocketed all of his or her own group of object balls and only needs to pocket the 8-ball (black) to win the game.

(c) Following the single free shot described in 6(a) the player's normal visit will commence.

7. LOSS OF THE GAME

Apart from the opponent playing a winning shot, a player can lose a game immediately by:

(a) pocketing the 8-ball (black) before pocketing all balls in his or her own group, except as allowed under Rule 4(g) (see page 49)

(b) going in off the 8-ball (black) when the 8-ball (black) is potted

(c) clearly failing to make any attempt to play a ball of his or her own group

(d) seeking to gain advantage by deliberately touching a moving ball or retrieving a ball dropping into the pocket.

The referee keeps a close eye on proceedings to ensure fair play.

8. GENERAL

The following is a list of additional general points.

(a) Push stroke This is when the tip of the cue remains in contact with the cue ball once it has commenced its forward motion.

(b) Cue ball in-hand When a player has the cue ball in-hand he or she plays from any position on or within the 'D' and in any direction.

(c) Player in control A player is said to be 'in control' of the table from the time that his or her body, cue or clothing touches the table prior to taking a shot, through the visit and up until the opponent does likewise prior to his or her visit. Any balls that fall into the pockets during this period (including 8-ball (black)), are considered potted by the player in control. The player in control is liable to any penalties or benefits normally awarded for the potting of that ball or balls according to the rules of the game (Rule 5(c) applies, see page 50).

▼ A player takes a shot at the cue ball to play it away from the object ball.

(d) The game is completed when the 8-ball (black) is potted in any pocket and all the remaining balls including the cue ball have come to rest, except where Rule 4(g) applies (see page 49).

(e) Touching ball A player must play away from a touching ball, which must not move (see Rule 5(s) on page 50). If the touching ball is one of the player's own group, he or she is deemed to have played that ball. If the touching ball is not one of the player's group, the cue ball must strike one of his or her own group. When Rule 6(b) applies a player must play away from a touching ball and is deemed to have played that ball (see page 51).

9. STALEMATE

If, for any reason, a legal shot cannot be played, then the game shall be re-started whether this situation is arrived at by accident or design. If the referee considers that neither player is allowing the game to progress or a stalemate situation has arisen, then the game shall be re-started.

FURTHER GUIDANCE

(a) The term 'shot' means striking the cue ball once.

(b) The term 'visit' refers to one turn at the table comprising one or a series of shots.

(c) The term 'break' refers to the first shot of the game or the first shot of a game being re-started.

(d) Coaching is deemed to be unsportsmanlike (see Rule 1 on page 48).

(e) A referee may, if requested, advise on rules of the game.

(f) There is an obligation on both players to ensure the breaking player nominates his group (see Rule 5(p) on page 50).

(g) The referee should ensure that no excessive time is taken to play a shot and act in accordance with competition guidance.

(h) Re-racks, as in Rule 9 above, may be with a reduced number of balls in accordance with competition rules and guidelines.

(i) In doubles matches, once a player is in control of the table, conversation with his or her partner is considered unsporting and shall be dealt with under competition rules.

BLACKBALL RULES

Although many casual pool games in pubs are played with 8-ball rules, the official rules are now known as the blackball rules. There are some subtle differences. Here is a summary of the blackball rules. Full details can be found online at www.poolpockets.co.uk.

BREAKING

- Lag to decide who breaks first, alternate breaks thereafter.

- Break from anywhere in baulk (behind the line).

- Legal break – two balls must pass the middle pockets or a ball must be potted.

- Penalty – one free shot, with a free table, plus one visit. May move cue ball to baulk and/or re-rack balls if desired.

- Blackball potted off break = re-rack, same player breaks.

DECIDING COLOURS

- The table is always open after the break shot regardless of what has been potted.

- The first legal pot on a visit (not a free shot) determines the colours.

- If balls of both colours are potted the table remains open.

- No nomination is necessary.

GENERAL PLAY

- Legal shot – A player must hit the cue ball and it must contact a ball of his own colour first (except after a foul). One or more balls must be potted and/or at least one ball must hit a cushion AFTER contact. Combination shots are allowed, i.e it is fine to pot one or more of your opponent's balls as long as you hit one of your balls first and one or more of your balls are potted in the same shot.

- A player's visit will continue until the player in control either fails to legally pot a ball of their own colour or commits a foul. Play will then pass to their opponent.

FOULS

- Potting the cue ball.

- Cue ball not hitting any ball.

- Cue ball contacting ball of opponent's colour or black first.

Exception: when you have a free table.

- Cue ball or another ball not hitting a cushion AFTER contacting a ball.
Exception: Unless you are snookered.

- Making any ball leave the table.

- Jumping over a ball.

- Touching any ball with anything except the tip of your cue.
Exception: when you have cue ball in-hand.

- Playing a push shot.

- Not playing a shot within 60 seconds – optional rule.

- The Penalty after a foul is one free shot with a free table. The player has the option to play the cue ball from where it lies or ask for it to be moved into baulk. The player then continues their visit.

FREE TABLE

- Player can hit, and/or pot, any ball. Can hit, but can't pot, the black.

LOSS OF FRAME FOULS

- Potting the black when not 'on' it.

- Potting the black with a foul shot.

- Playing a 'deliberate' foul.

- Touching the cue ball when you do not have ball in-hand.

STALEMATE

- If it is not possible for a legal shot to be played then the frame shall be re-started.

WINNING

- A player wins by legally potting all their balls plus the black. They may pot their last ball(s) and the black in the same shot.

OTHER POOL GAMES

There are various other fun and exciting games that can be played on a standard pool table. These include speed pool, best shot, on the green, golf, diamond nine and survivor. The basic rules for these games are shown in this final section of the book. Why not try your hand at one or all of them – and give it your best shot!

SPEED POOL

The object of this game is to pot all the balls in the fastest time.

Competition

1. Players enter their names in any space available in one of any 'heat'.

2. Players have three turns in finding their fastest time, and write their time for each turn in the boxes by their name for their heat.

3. In each heat, players can either have their three turns consecutively, or we recommend that each player plays alternately.

4. When all players have had their three turns in a heat, the fastest time is the heat winner.

Rack the balls as for basic pool.

5. The four heat winners then compete to decide the champion.

Speed pool rules

1. Nominate a timekeeper for the frame.

2. Once the timekeeper says 'go', the clock starts ticking. When the last ball is potted, the clock stops.

3. The player can pot any ball in any order (including black).

4. If the cue ball is potted or comes off the table, it is re-spotted in the 'D'.

5. If any other ball comes off the table it is re-spotted on the head spot or as near to it as possible in a line from the head spot to the centre of the 'D'.

6. Only the player on the table may pick up and replace balls as in (4) and (5) above; the penalty is the time taken to do this.

7. In the event of a tie, the players concerned take one turn each until there is a winner.

A player tries to beat the clock in a fast and furious game of speed pool.

BEST-SHOT COMPETITION

The object of this game is to pot all the balls using the least number of shots.

How to play

1. This game is played over three frames. Count for each frame the number of shots taken to pot all balls in any order. Your lowest score is used to decide your position. (Ask a friend to keep score.)

2. There are four heats; enter in one only.

3. When all names are entered on to the match sheet, commence the competition.

4. Each of the heat winners will play off to find out who is really the best shot.

5. In the event of a tie, play a deciding frame.

Who's the best shot? A non-player keeps a note of the number of strokes taken to pot all the balls.

ON THE GREEN (NINE BALLS)

The object of this game is to pot a ball in each pocket with the lowest number of strokes.

How to play

1.

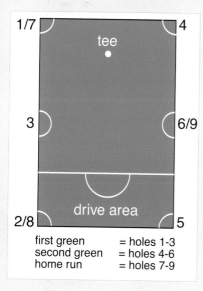

first green	= holes 1-3
second green	= holes 4-6
home run	= holes 7-9

On the green.

2. Start with the first putter (player) on the first green. The putter places one ball on the tee and putts (pots) it into hole number 1. The next ball on the tee goes to hole number 2 and the next on to hole number 3. Move then to the second green, starting at hole number 4, followed by number 5 and then number 6. You putt the last three balls (the home run) starting at hole number 7 and ending at hole number 9.

3. In the 'rough' (foul): Foul shots incur the following penalties.

- If you pocket the white add a stroke to your score.

- If you putt into the wrong hole add three strokes to your score.

- If you run out of balls for your remaining holes add five strokes to your score for each hole that you cannot putt a ball into.

4. When all nine balls are putted, add up your strokes and then the next putter putts.

5. Tie: In the event of a tie, play for hole number 3. There should be one ball per player and the lowest score wins.

Balls are set up with the white ball in 'D' and one other ball on the centre spot (the 'tee').

The winner is whoever has the lowest score.

GOLF (NINE BALLS)

The object of this game is to pot a ball in each pocket within the allowed number of 'goes' ('par').

> **Set up the nine balls in a diamond, in any order.**

How to play

1. Each hole has a number of 'goes' allowed (par).

2. Golf balls are putted (potted) in any order. However, you nominate each ball for the pocket and must putt it in that pocket. Start on the first green with par 1 pockets, then on to par 2 pockets, and then par 3 pockets; then on to the second green.

3. When six balls have been putted, pocket the last three – each in a different par pocket.

4. In the 'rough' (foul): The following penalties are incurred for foul strokes.

- If you pocket the white add a stroke to your score.

- If you putt into the wrong hole add the par value to your score.

- If you run out of balls for your remaining holes up to ball number 6 use the hole par value as your score. For balls 7, 8 and 9 – add three per ball plus the whole par value as your score.

5. After the first golfer has potted nine balls, the second golfer starts. Take the table par value from your total number of strokes to get your net score.

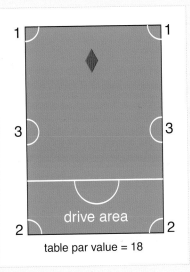

table par value = 18

 Golf.

> **The winner is the 'golfer' with the lowest net score.**

DIAMOND NINE (NINE BALLS)

The object of diamond nine is to pot the numbered balls from 1 to 9 consecutively.

How to play

1. Hit the lowest numbered ball first. If this is pocketed, you score one point. Then try to pocket the next lowest numbered ball for one point. Continue to play each consecutive ball in turn until you fail to pocket a ball or make a diamond Lil (foul)! Your opponent then gains control of the table.

2. Diamond Lil! If you pocket or hit the wrong number, pot the white, or miss a ball completely, the next player places the white ball anywhere.

3. Scoring. You score one point for each correctly potted ball, but whoever pockets the number 9 (if it is still on the table) last gets an extra five points!

Rack the balls in a diamond shape with number 9 in the middle, number 1 at the front, and the white ball in the 'D'.

The winner is whoever scores the most points.

SURVIVOR

The object of this game is to be the last player (or survivor) on the table.

How to play

1. Any number of players may enter.

2. Players play alternately.

3. Each player has three 'lives'.

4. A player on his or her turn has to pot a ball (any ball including the 8-ball black) – except the cue ball.

5. If a player fails to pot a ball, he loses a 'life'. If a player loses three 'lives' he or she is out.

6. If a player pots the cue ball, goes in off, or causes a ball to leave the table, he or she loses a life.

7. Any ball off the table is placed as near the head spot as possible. The cue ball is placed in the 'D'.

8. When the last ball is potted and there is more than one survivor remaining, the balls are re-racked and the next player on breaks.

9. At all times the player who breaks has an extra shot.

Rack the balls for basic pool.

A player fights to be the last one standing in a game of survivor.

INDEX